AF255186

Written by Sue Dickson
Books For Hope
booksforhope.co.nz

More books by Sue
Inner Peace - What does inner peace mean to you?
The Little Prayer Book
Wisdom - Your message to the world
Power of the Heart - Affirmations
Happiness Is...

Graphic Design by Conor Seed
theseeds.co.nz

Photos by Danny Yates

Catholic Art Images of Paintings
www.restoredtraditions.com

Edited by Emma Seed

ISBN 978-0-473-46664-0

W·BOVGVEREAV·1903

A very special heartfelt thank you to Danny Yates, and Restored Traditions for their photos and paintings. Much love to you both.

I dedicate this book to Emma and Conor Seed.

I am so blessed to have my beautiful daughter, Emma Seed, and my wonderful son-in-law, Conor Seed, involved with Books for Hope. Without you both, this organisation would not exist. Your dedication, time, effort, love and support is very much appreciated. I cannot put into words what this means for me and the children. From my heart and soul, thank you.

Readers, I hope this book inspires you to look within and see the good inside yourself. May it affirm your value and significance and, most of all, remind you that the world is a better place with you in it.

Lots of love,

Sue Dickson

Hope and Love

W·BOVGVEREAV·1899

Love gives hope.

Love is faithful.

Love is powerful.

Love is the future of mankind and peace.

Spread the word of peace.

Spread the word of hope.

Spread the world of love.

Spread the word of forgiveness.

Spread the word of God.

Peace will follow.

Rise above negativity.

See the good within.

Then radiate love to all mankind.

You are a beauitful flower that blossoms in the sun.

Sending love and hope to everyone today.

May your heart be filled with joy.

May you be open to change.

May you rejoice in the fact that you are valued, worthy and loved.

Never give up.

Your strength and wisdom are more powerful than you realise.

Today is a gift.

Use it wisely - spread hope and love.

Love is the key to peace.

Be at peace with yourself.

Be at peace with others.

Be at peace with God.

Be at peace with humanity.

Then your world will transform.

Shine your light wherever you go.

Be grateful for the little things in life.

They amount to the big things that matter.

You never walk alone.

God has your back.

Walk with courage.

Walk with compassion.

Walk with joy.

Walk with love.

Walk with freedom.

And the world belongs to you.

SHARE
THE ROAD

You are the power - you are the light that shines within.

Gratitude is the source of love that comes from the soul.

Forgiveness is the price we pay for freedom and inner peace.

Laugh and dance as if you are a child -

With freedom, passion and no judgement.

Children are everything.

Tell your children they are loved,

they are valued,

they matter,

and they are worthy of your love.

Tell them about the joy they bring,

the hope and love they give you,

the rainbow of sunshine, happiness, fulfilment and purpose

they bring to your life each and every day.

Be kind to nature.

Spend as much time in nature as you can;

it is good for your mind, body, and soul.

Pets are a great source of comfort.

Music is a powerful force.

Always have faith that you are in the right place doing what God has planned for you.

You can do this. He has chosen you for a reason.

Never doubt your vision, your passion, your courage, your strength, your wisdom or your faith.

You are strong and you are loved.

This is what God sees in you.

Treat people the way you would like to be treated.

W. BOUGUEREAU

A smile can change a person's world.

Love can change the universe.

You are important.

You matter.

The world is a better place with you in it.

Cherish every day as if it was your last.

Treasure your friends and family.

They are worth all the gold and silver in the universe.

Today I am sending you joy, love and healing.

Love and accept yourself - this is the key to peace within.

One person can make a difference in the world.

Don't be afraid to be that person. Trust that you have the skills, the courage, determination and love to be that person.

I pray that you receive love, happiness, good health, freedom, healing and God's love.

May your journey be filled with love and light.

W.BOVGVEREAV.1900